I UNDERSTAND AND
I WISH TO CONTINUE

poetry by

Travis R. Venters

MAIN STREET RAG PUBLISHING COMPANY
CHARLOTTE, NORTH CAROLINA

Acknowledgments:
> *The Main Street Rag:* "Community Legends," "That Old Time
>   Relgion," "Ten Day Drunk," "Taking The Local Home."
> *Iodine Poetry Journal*: " Before I Moved To Japan"
> *The Greensboro Review:* "Beside A River"
> *The Massachusetts Review:* " Anniversary"
> *Tokyo Metropolis:* " Night Thunder, Suginami-ku," "Senso-Ji"

Earlier versions of some of the poems have appeared in other
magazines in Japan. May they rest in peace.

I wish to thank Scott Douglass for his patience and wisdom;
Heather Ross Miller for years of encouragement and just being
clear headed about the poetry biz; Maria Domoto for her heavy
duty patience; also, Max Steele, Fred Chappell, John Gribble, and
Paul Rossiter, and lastly Robert Watson.

ISBN: 978-1-59948-431-0

Produced in the United States of America

Main Street Rag
PO Box 690100
Charlotte, NC 28227
www.MainStreetRag.com

For: *Angus Lindsey*
Sean StandingBear
Bob Holland
Rocco Sorrenti
Kamiriyo Sensei
Michael Cusamano
Raleigh Powell
Jim Peacock
Masa Adachi
Richard Gatling
Thomas Yellowtail

My brothers and mentors.

Contents

America

Japan

Blind Man On The Beach and Other Poems

AMERICA

RED NECK EGOIST

Jack Daniels really throws a rope.
I get roped most every Saturday night.

I tell the little lady if she don't like it
Hell, that's fine. I'll just get another filly.

But I try to make it to Mt Carmel Baptist
And dressed upright in shoes that bite.

Saw the preacher at the Post Office,
Asked him which was faster prayer or air mail?

Prayer, he says. Well, like the rest of us
He can only guess. He's just more uncomfortable.

Even though he has a job to do, I told him
Not to worry over much about my soul.

God is my second cousin twenty-six
Times removed on my mother's side.

He looked at me with such bug eyed disbelief
 I felt like an occupational hazard.

I know the Sermon on the Mount is true
But I listen better with a brew.

AN ELDERLY WOMAN

On the Washington Mall grabs my arm
And whispers, *When blue try wearing red.*

But white guys are terrible in red trousers
Except when they are playing golf.

Mt cotton top head treasures such details.
My life is full of stories soaked in red:

A girl friend whose father sold her violin
To buy coke wishing he would die.

Asking my brother about his first date,
He mutters hydrangeas give better head.

My wife admitting that until she burned her bra
She felt pressured by things as they are.

She has gone back to the bra and I have gone
Back to her. We don't whisper any more.

COMMUNITY LEGENDS

Dick soon tired of his running and lived
For the day he could drive. See Dick drive
His Daddy's Bonneville off to Cherry Grove.
Se Dick dance to "It Will Stand" and "Stay"
His highlight moments of his high school years.
So anyway whatever happened to Dick? you ask.
Went missing.1968. Second tour. Hue, Viet Nam.
Body not recovered. Came back a flag.

Jane always had these extraordinary legs.
All us boys liked to see Jane run, see her panties
White as milk. Oh the colors they promised us.
See Jane as Spring in a local Balanchine, a handy
Russian passion produced for our local Methodists.
All of us wanted her but there was always one
Everybody wants and Jane left no goodbyes.
What could have changed our gap tooth gazelle?
The girls wanted us to know but wouldn't tell.

Spot had a bastard's bloodline, one show dog
Two sires back on his mother's side, but damn
That dog could hunt! Why is a mutt like a hero?
No brainier for a boy. Show me the girl
Who can run a rabbit, tree a coon, or kill a snake
Or howl at the moon half as fast, and I'll call my
Congressman, Dick's favorite receiver in those days,
Who will soon announce he won't run again.
Bad health. Declining wealth, and I'll say *Buddy*
Have I got the candidate for you down here on Little Creek.
Spot met his maker chasing a Merita bread truck.
I cried and cried. I cried a lot. But like my Daddy
Liked to say, *Wes all gots to go sometime.*

UNDER SMALL TOWN LIGHTS

You father a small boy said to be pretty like his mother.
Then you go get killed in the war; I became our teacher's pet.
Older boys hated that odd attention. I learn their meanness.
Come football, freshman year, I benched a senior.

After that people didn't care if I like poems or painting.
I took social dancing and played trombone. Oh, sore lips.
A blue-eyed girl whose possibilities rescued me from cars
Took me unto the fields of clover. We recreated happiness.

Boys like me learn on the wing the *most important* things.
We learn encouragement comes from inner courage.
We learn to be a little horrible, for survival isn't free.
Even so father, there were moments we met

In my privacy of my football helmet and taped hands:
Those father/son nights when before the coin toss
The team would take the fifty yard line. When a name
Was called, a father stands and accepts the public toast.

I held my helmet up when my name was called.

After we all ran back to our sideline I would
Stare across the field to find the boy I had to beat
Or face humiliation, my fear in smash mouth yardage.
No matter what the pain, playing through pain made

Me feel in your world. I loved knocking down
The boys of men who made it back to the mills.
Our blood mingled in the red zone. Win or lose,
No one whapped my back or shook my hand.

I held my helmet over my head to where you are.

MUTTERING PIGEONS

Poor humans. All that effort. We pigeons have it easy.
When it comes to being global, we follow money and don't get lost.
Our portfolios are the envy of all the other birds in town.
Our investments are prudent so we are secure. Currency, no problem.
Our major differences are minor. We are not blue jays or cardinals.
Public life and private matters create no conflicts of interest.
We enjoy a universal language. Our poetry is vowel based.
Rhyme is easy. Street wisdom, you say. Well, we invented it.
Pigeons don't drink to excess, or fornicate without reason.
We do not stay angry at our fathers and never ever commit suicide.
We talk with spirits. We sing with angels. Poor humans,
As you do unto the least of us, you do to you.

HONOR GUARDS

Wait for the hearse.
Spring storms have blown shingles
Off the church roof. But what is this
To the deacon to be buried?

There is not enough of the old congregation
To hold a decent service. Most relatives
Arriving with the hearse are visitors.

I am the last member of our choir.
The others are sealed in bronze
Six feet down.

Two altos, short stuffy women,
Lived to out sing each other. Their
Head stones keep the secret.

Pot bellied sergeants dress a line.
One steps out to give commands
And the rifles come up. Pow. Pow. Pow.

His sons and their children
Shift weight from foot to foot
While the Captain folds the flag.

Do his grandchildren know
He loved to take his horse and buggy
Down the hill to get his mail.

Cars and trucks be damned.

ANNIVERSARY

Remember the night we were zooming across
Kansas and you said I hadn't said anything for
An hour and it was getting creepy so what was
I really thinking? You were waving your arm
Out the window saying *hello moon, hello stars*
Like they ought to hello you, too; but at that very
Moment you were also a nude starlet on your mother's
Bed sheets. So we blew through Wichita wondering
What tattoo would look good at the base of your back,
What you called your basic high dive platform.
You wanted a red arrow from your ass up your spine
To the nape of your neck. You said that would empty
All the swimming pools in Baltimore. Even now the very
Thought of you can make driving in the dark
An aboriginal adventure. I hope this card
Makes it into your hands.

BOY'S OWN ADVENTURES

There I was on the mountain top
Helping the settlers make their getaway
Holding off the entire Shawnee nation
With my trusty long rifle and my famous
Ability to shoot fifty balls a minute

There I was diving off a Missouri river boat
Into the roiling murk to catch a lady's
Gold watch, an heirloom, all that is left
Of her daddy's plantation, because I won
Her in a card game _____

There I was the last U.S. sailor left alive
On a south pacific isle where I gather up
Coconuts to serve to a desperate company
Of nurses commanded by a red headed major
Who cries in my arms _____

Here I am in a hospital that smells
Like Wal Mart when the Doctor comes in
With his game face on, leans in my direction,
His chest covered by my chart, and says
You have cancer _____

Here I will be the last person to leave
The vast library built between my ears.
My hands will be full of unread books
And paperclips from the Circulation desk.
I will leave all the lights on. _____

THAT OLD TIME RELIGION

Here in bee season
Air thick with barnyard smells
Our ancient organ shrieks
Like a heat rash gone to hell
Across the congregation
Gathered here to bury our neighbor.
The mortician has worked his
Mighty wonders to behold
For later comers who need
An open coffin. One last look
Then songs, prayers over,
The Director leans over
And folds her bifocals.
Resting them on her cheek,
He touches her chin, then darkness.
Her youngest son begins
To chirp like a baby bird.
As we march out
Into the broiling sun,
Someone behind us begins
To sing *Beulah Land.*
She is heavy on our shoulders.
What I'd give for a cool breeze.

BEFORE I MOVED TO JAPAN

One night in Carrboro

She said, "That was not sex.
That was the feeling of California
Falling off into the ocean."

Senior spring came
I still didn't have a comeback.
Then it was too late.

She'd moved on to Arizona.

JAPAN

SOMETHING OF NOTHING

A thick sun ray by a waterfall
Cuts cloud to the edge of a red temple
Where mind and body fall apart.
Rainbows glisten on the monks

Gathered there for tea and sweets.
We cannot see how they see the sun.
Their holy gossip lives without us
Unless we join them in the mist.

WAITING IN A KICHIJOJI CAFE

Beside my table
Hangs a child's water color:

In the park
A man is walking
All is lemon green in his world

The man might be a father

He is alone with his loneliness
The sky is working hard to be blue
He will disappear

When he chases the pigeons away.

That child
Did he have a place to go
Or like me

Just simply go.

OVER THE WALL IN KABUKI CHO

The Roshi says there are clouds
In my sky so I mustn't stop my work.

My old friend tells me on her weekend break.
We have decided on a movie. A decent date

Even here in the guts of Kabuki- Cho.
Her knees creak from weeks of zazen.

I guess I am her worldly friend.
For me renunciation is a lark.

Before us like a topsail full of wind
Is an advertisement, a painted banner

Of a woman on her knees, her mouth is open
A perfect invitation to fellatio.

Don't you think all that is silly?
No. Not silly. Not sad. Not good.

Not bad. One more knot
In Buddha's scarlet thread.

ENGLISH AS A SECOND LANGUAGE

A mosquito coil burns in the corner
On the low wooden table. Letters from home
In the candlelight look white as apple blossoms.

My sweetheart has a tiny mole
Just left of her Angel's ladder.
Below is musk of oranges and new earth.

We are resting as lovers did in Heian times.
The fields are planted and so we talk of the weather
Our bodies might make.

There are precedents: Gauguin, Lafcadio Hearn, but not Pierre Loti.
I wonder if I have cashed out commonsense.
From now on its gold coins and silver bangles.

Like the smoke over there her voice floats off the pillow
Are we difficult? I'm sorry. I meant to say different.
I answer, *No not unless you want to be.*

NIGHT THUNDER IN SUGINAMI, TOKYO

Buckets of water slam rooftops.
The windows and the sliding doors all shake.
The ones who remember burrow deeper into sleep.

Sleep is only a presence. The elders bend into the wind
And carry buckets of weightless water up onto roofs.
The B-29s are back bringing a thousand fires.

Why believe: *They died peacefully in their sleep?*
They don't wake up and tell us their dreams.

DINNER PARTY IN KAMAKURA

An invitation I cannot refuse
Brings me to a house not too far
From where Kawabata killed himself.
Not even Donald Keene knows why.

Sea breezes meander off the bay.
Potently full of wine and cheese, faces
Glow like red lanterns at twilight.
A whisper of Moonlight Sonata at 4 p.m.

Voices: Thank you, how are you doing?
Thank you. How about you?
There she is the Dean's daughter,
Full force fox, my student.

Keep the rules: a full glass, nibble,
Talk like you mean it. Smile a lot.
Don't leave too soon. Pray hard
Your name survives the day.

BESIDE A RIVER

Egg shell evening light
Notes of a temple bell
Down river in bamboo.

A dragon fly hovers nearby.
We share brown rice tea
From a handy thermos.

Shall we keep the child?

Your eyes
Track a young monk
On his way to a meal.

In the distance
I hear a car horn.
We can't hitch a ride.

We shall keep the child.

ATAMI

Cats in sunshine
On the grey tiles of the sushi bar roof
Remind me again of my deepest desires,
Never really asleep, just resting
Plotting their next moves.

TEN DAY DRUNK

For Ikkyu Sojun

I splash my face with too much Bermuda lime after shave
While the person in the mirror demands I take him to my leader.
At this moment I see my face before I was born. There is
Nothing I can do. This person looking back is on his own.

Smoking lamp is lit. Fifteen years in the Baptist church.
Ten years on Tokyo streets begging for invisible tattoos.
I have three college degrees. I have put down bad guys
And have saved a few lives. I have twice survived divorce.

When hungry eat, but feed the hungrier first.
When sleepy, sleep, but first see to it that all may sleep in safety.
When angry, shout; when sad, cry. When calm, be calm.
Be gentle with what you earn. Death comes. Life comes.

        So what about so what.

KOFU TO ASAGAYA BY RAIL

My train pulls out of Kofu
Soon rolls past a red pagoda rising
Above an ocean of grapes waving bye-bye.
Bye-bye. On the horizon five clouds inch
Over mountain trails I have yet to explore.
I am more your typical urban recluse.
My city six mat room is remote as any cave.
We stop at Enzan and hikers hustle on
With sunburns the scent of soy sauce.
A few hours later, in Tokyo, I get off at Asagaya,
I am just at the station wicket when a snaggle
Toothed lady with wild grey hair, a strand in her mouth,
Throws a hand in my face. *STOP!* She wears two warm up suits
And a scarf with a pattern of giraffes.

American? Yes, American, I think, but you look so German.
Well too bad. OK. Here is a song for you.
Angel boy. Angel boy. Try to smile. Try to smile.
La la. La la. Just for a while, Try to smile.
I'll brush your hair for just a while. La la. La la.
Now you'll sleep tonight. Sleep with angels, angel boy.

Then in a flash she is gone.
Hand to my head I stagger off
Into a swirl of happy drunks
And get in the taxi line.

KANDA BOOKSTORE

Stop in a shop and open a book:
A photograph taken off a dead Japanese.
An execution in China, late thirties.

He was a man, no name, no matter.
Cutting off heads is what I do best
Ask any of the other officers.

The usual crowd gathers:
Cooks. Coolies. Off duty privates.
The curious on their way home.

Everybody keeps a distance to avoid
The blood gush from the neck.
Smiles all round.

There is one fat European
With his camera. I hear the shutter
With the swish of my keen sword

And the quick shout

Yaaaa. A clean cut!

KANDA CAFE

The food is two stars and student cheap
But half the customers have towels around their heads
And jika-tabi on their feet. They stare at me

Taking a break from buying books
In another part of the neighborhood. These men
Are helping Tokyo disappear, the Tokyo

Rebuilt after 1945. The pot stickers
Are sumptuous but a little onion heavy. A shrine
Guards a television where underage girls

Sing and wiggle in frilly fuck me suits
That actually make the sticky rice taste better.
Professors and day laborers, appetite unites us all.

* Jika-tabi are split toed footwear favored by construction workers.

SLOW DAY IN GINZA

(ching, ching)

Desire for an end to desire?
You might just as well spend your days
Hanging your head over to hear the wind blow.

Somewhere between good faith and bad
We all do our part; even this Buddhist beggar
With his big black bowl.

Oh Monk without cushion,
Did you laugh before your father had a face?
Do you secretly yearn for a trip to Hawaii?

I drop a fist of coins into his bowl,
His blessing goes in one ear and out the other.
We wait for the light to change.

(ching, ching)

TAKING THE LOCAL HOME

Coming back from a teacher's conference
I catch the last train out of Odawara.
Across from me a silver haired lady stares
In and out the window. A salary man
 Publically performs the fact he is her son.
They discuss the cancer that burns
Beneath her black and gold kimono.
She speaks softly to her reflection.
He replies with a greater urgency,
Debating which train their relatives
Must take home after her cremation.
He insists his way is faster.

A WIDOW PAYS HER RESPECTS

The white doves here at Yasukuni
Kicking about in the rusty cherry leaves
Remind me of your white gloves.
I take a deep breath and slowly exhale.
What you have become, I will be.
To fortify myself before my visit
I did the girlish thing of having cake
With tea. The tea was exquisite.
You once whispered a navy officer
Should not love cake. I remember
Laughing at our secret. Chocolate Éclair!
Banzai! Chocolate éclair! Banzai!

SENSO-JI

The Sumida river sparkles with spring highlights
And dank scents too dark and down for temple incense.
Once the river was iced with bodies charred by fire.

Children play hide and seek near the bridge.
They don't care.

An old woman waits for the light, her back
Bent with a basket of cabbages for the cutlet houses.
She doesn't care.

Two pretty girls with crooked teeth carry their loud
Laughter into the public bath house. They work tonight.
They don't care.

A high school boy tends to his aggressive pompadour.
His uniform is missing a few buttons. He has no books.
He doesn't care.

Around this tourist temple
Tens of thousands of Japanese vanished in a fire storm.
They don't care.

Two police men ride by on bicycles
Business as usual.

THE PAST FOR POSTAGE

A letter arrives from Sapporo.
She writes *Do you remember me?*
Six years ago you gave me panties
You had painted pink roses on by hand.
Can you get into the sweater I knitted?
I have become a teacher too. As good as you
But not as bold as you. I am a good wife too.
One son. One daughter. One husband.
Remember me? Good. Now forget.

OK

I put ice cubes in a glass
To melt with Super Nikka whiskey;
Ignore warnings and take a sleeping pill.
I use a small towel in place of pajamas.
Its weight upon my genitals
Soft as her hand.

KAMAKURA BAY

Yellow clouds of sand slowly
Blow across Kamakura bay.
Thank you Red China.

The bay is off limits to U.S.
Navy famlies due to fecal bacteria.
The locals can't read the warning sign.

I wander past shops: fruits, grains,
Greens, meats fish, and tourist do-dads.
Tourist prosperity has become postwar work,

Visible signs of Banzai recovery.
In this ancient capital history resides
In local tofu, rice, eggplants and cabbage.

Legends tell of whole families put to sword
Here in these dunes where couples like to snuggle.
People buy. Buy some more. Then they die.

The status of forces agreement does not apply.

WAR POEM

Saigon fell. I was teaching a class.
On the streets business men
Told me I had lost.

I let student mistakes
Be sleeping dogs:

Akiko from snow country wrote
I am like glass with no roots.

Sonoko from Hiroshima wrote
The Japanese political system is likewise a cow.

Akira from a Chiba peanut patch wrote
Cage gathering people like to feed the monkeys.

Flash to when the towers burn and bodies fly.
From the back of another classroom a male voice shouts
Are you proud of being an American?

I shout, *Are you proud of being a Japanese?*
He shouts again, *I don't know. I'm only an economics major.*

KICHIJOJI STARBUCKING

For Rocco Sorrenti

Sweet bun sugar
The light sweat
On that girl's neck
Makes me ache.

(Yeats, Eliot, Goethe, and Ikkyu are my precedents.)

Hosei high school boys
Stroll by and their sport club bags
Bump their tiny wallet catwalk butts.
Girl gangs follow fresh off the elevators
And the sales at Isetan. Smell good going up.
Smell good going down.

Department store bags
Are like bras around here.
Few know what waits inside.

God and the Devil are talking shop.
Women shall have the curse. What shall we do to men?
Give them endless desires for women they can never know.
The shop talk continues. Maybe it's raining.
God asks *How shall we shape the American character?*
Devil says *What do YOU think?*

God says *We keep those continents out of all the Books*
We make greed available in attractive forms of slavery
And give them lots of wars.

In Tokyo white pigeons stand for peace
At the most arrogant Shrine for dead soldiers.

White socks stand for the edgy pink energy of
Junior high school beings. The young girls are multiples
Of what passes here for mom and apple pie.

In the year I was born Tokyo burned
But not here, not in Kichijoji.
Blame it on the weather. Curtis did.

Death by fire is a promise given unto us by God;
Yet we pray for help when parking our cars.
Our Lord must love our jokes.

I am really getting too old for Tokyo.
My wife shouts *Did you really sleep with all those girls?*
I want to say *Yes!* But I can't remember.

In 1972 my body collects girl bodies
Then one night my skinny disco babe rolls over
And says very clearly *Make me your boy.*
The religious art of East and West
Center on the same concentrations of frenzy, joy,
And suffering inch by pretty inch.

Say yes scholar, or be damned to hell.

The Buddha sat because the tree
Didn't come with a chair, nor did he have
Football knees. *Jukai* came later.

Islam is to be disrespected at your peril these days
But in Tokyo so is shopping. Live better; buy more.
Improve reality as you can. The we of *We Japanese.*

One expat friend is dead. Another has moved to Manila.
It is so impossible to be a nihilist in Tokyo. Too many cynics.
My country drunk or sober. Roll on, barrels of *sake*. Roll.

Three coffees. Three Starbucks. Same Kichijoji.
My soul has turned Japanese by half. Like a magic free
Tissue pack, always another tissue left.

(Thank you street girl with orange hair and silver nose ring.)

I don't worry myself with blasphemy
When I was five our Lord whispered in my ear
I will make you unhappy so you can make me laugh.

One table over a woman reads
A glossy magazine on knitting.
She is rubbing a long elegant finger
Up and down the side of her nose.

A few hours away
Snow, ocean,
The enemy.

IKKYU

Says writing poetry is a waste of time
But being old and feeling a more urgent need for merit
I ask the enlightened lecher what to do. He says *Go write*
More poetry. Make it as fun as women.

OVIDIAN APHORISMS

For Quanah

Love is every person's introduction to chaos theory.

What fate cannot change, neither can plastic surgery.

Sex is the best argument that might be made for intelligent design.

The first kiss may be stolen. But steal wisely for the second kiss
    May prove fatal, or worse.

When you must go, leave. Don't demand gratitude for going.

The golden mean is much appreciated by scholars, and this is
    Wise on their part. Even so, seek for wiser women.

When your wife and your mother start to talk about your childhood
    Take your dog for a walk.

Before you marry, think through the issues of property.
    Likely you will die first; No man needs to encourage this.

Never kill yourself when a woman fails to find
    You loveable. Why endorse her point of view?

Don't show your lover images of sexual congress until she
    Cannot be surprised.

The giving of gifts, of chocolates, of tickets to spectacles is much
    Loved by young girls. Not by their fathers.

Sometimes you have to shoot back at Cupid. Never aim to kill
    But to create some caution within his mischief.

Say: go far, as far as you dream, sweet peach.
    But take me too; I am the earth that feeds your branch.

Beware of wanting to be interesting, or a character around town.
    You have to fuck up a lot to achieve this honor.

Memorize this. Make it the central truth of your marriage.
    When I miss you, nothing else matters.

No matter what the physicians say,
    You can die from over exposure to beauty.
.
The opposite of sex is not abstinence.
    It is nausea.

Take care of her needs first;
    Her first needs are also yours.

HOW I MET YOUR MOTHER

For Keiko Takahata

I found my new frontier in Tokyo
Few white people, cheap beer, tatami burns.
One Saturday night outside a movie theater
A drunk attacks me with a long kitchen knife.
Swinging the blade he shouts *I want to kill Americans.*
I was alone and fleet of foot. When I think
About it, his English skills were nearly perfect.
Your mother was weeks away from meeting me.

         One night

A stranger in a trench coat stood in front of me
One homesick evening on the train to Kichijoji
To get my pumpkin pie at an America pie shop.
I was nodding off when this guy screams *Hiroshima,*
Hiroshima, Nagasaki, Hiroshima then this girl
Jumped up and punched him in the jaw. I thought
This one is way above the rest. At the station,
Holding hands we got off the train.

BLIND MAN ON THE BEACH
AND OTHER POEMS

BLIND MAN ON THE BEACH

My name is Doolin. I find myself
Without much up or down but with my feet
Connected to this sand and the surf
That tells me here I stand.
Isn't it a lovely day? Got a cigarette?
Thanks. I have to sneak.
My wife is a hell of a lady but she won't
Buy me no cancer sticks. My dog here
Would if she could. Damn fine dog.
I lost my sight in 67 in a hot LZ
In the highlands. I remember the flash
But I can't see it no more. The last
Week before I went to basic, my brother
Gave me the use of his white Impala
With the red leather seats. Me and her
Came down here and we stood barefoot
And made our promises. Find me a man
In the White House that's done that.
We got drunk some, rode the ferris wheel,
And we danced some. The shag.
It Will Stand and *Carolina Girls*
When I got out of the VA hospital
She said *Doolin, you know what I look like*
And I know you so don't let your injury injure me.
She is very much the plus side of my life.
But friend if we have time for another smoke
I would be much obliged. Thanks.
Some will tell a person that the ocean
Makes them feel small, or lonely. They ask me
What is the point of it? Me looking out there. I say
We blind folks got plenty to hide too, the same right
To ponder infinity or death and taxes as any sighted man.

I hate the words *visually impaired.* I am stone cold fucking blind.
Blind have our own finesse. Take my word for it.
Love the sound of the waves and the feel of water on my ankles.
Love to smell the breeze and all that is more than them
That just look at the water. Waist deep is bold adventure
For that crowd. No I'm not bitter, just factual.
My wife expects my body
To be whole again when I stand before the Saints
Don't you know that will be a dazzling day
Since I can't take these Ray Bans with me.
Sure. I understand. Well, nice talking to you.
Time is precious. I wouldn't waste much of it
Worrying about river boats or rich boys.
There are the fortunate sons, and then there is us.
That there is all I know about history.
Everybody lies about Nam. There it is.
Thank you kindly for the smokes.

DOOLIN A LITTLE WIRED ON BUD

You mind? I ain't sober and I ain't not drunk.
A blind man can't get blind drunk, but wired, oh yes.
Bartender said you was here. Please keep your seat.
Haven't seen you since high school. I share
My table with any good soul that needs a seat.
You are a still good soul now, ain't you?
You'll always look the same to me. Not that it mattes,
My wife says that's a good thing for most of the guys
Living around here, we so busy checking out
The ladies, we don't notice much self-decline.
No, she is not here. Never took joy in John's Tavern.
Doing this just to be doing it is not on her list of things
We have to get done before we die. But it is on mine.
I was raised in a temperance household; grandma used to say
"Snakes teeth in every bowl" beer or wine. I sneaked to drink.
Don't you think I'm here making up for being good.
 Can't make up for nothing and that is a fact. But
I like the sounds and smells of most any juke joint.
There is a heavy texture to it I didn't notice when I was
Sighted; you ought to try getting high when there is
No up or down or left or right. Budweiser the equalizer.
I heard you spent a lot of time overseas. Church work
People say. True? Educational missionary! Well, we need
That stuff right here. It's pretty foreign right here.
Half of Mexico living in my back yard right now!

You get obligated to the VA hospital, and what are the options
And your heart itself is liable to go blind. My wife was what
Saved me. She says it was Jesus. It was the comfort of her voice.
I like to have me some beers, eat me some pickled eggs,
Listen to the guys bullshit, and pretty soon I feel back
To where I feel connected with my other life.

My wife says if I hate what is going on so much, run for office?
Well, honey, I say, *I don't want to be responsible for the blind*
Leading the blind. Washington is bad enough as it is.

You say you like Japan. I was a few days in a hospital
Somewhere in Tokyo, Camp Zama, me and my Purple Heart.
No, don't worry. If you ain't had your own share
Of bad shit, you will. Just happens. All else is lies.
You been to the Wall up there in Washington?
Get your ass on up there. It's perfect as those things go.
You was a hippie? Well don't let that stop you. I was a hippie, too.
Had them love beads. Had that peace sign on my helmet.

We had a college boy on our fire team. Got busted for half
An ounce. Judge knew his dad. Said you enlist and I never saw
You standing there. Or you can play basketball ten years inside.
A smart ass at first but steady under fire. He's on the Wall.
One night we was on guard duty and whispering about what we
Loved, what we missed, what we wanted back in the world.
I was talking about my brother's Chevy, one tricked out beast.
And he confesses he likes philosophy. I felt real sorry for that guy.
Here he was double lost in a starless cluster fuck.
We go deeper and he give me a good reason for why
We weren't going to win that war. It was the essence of Cong.

We never saw the Cong on any regular basis. Killed a few.
Even so, he said, *we'd never defeat, the Congless Cong.*
Since we couldn't understand their essence, the ideal
Cong, he said we'd never save what wasn't there to be saved.
Well he got his shit blown away while sleeping in a hole
At a firebase by a bad luck mortar round. Chance is a bitch.
I always have a philosophical beer when I come to John's.
You only need to go to that Wall once and then you can take
It with you anywhere. Forever if you want to. My wife put my fingers
On a few of the names. Future generations ought to study the wall.

I wanted to rub some chicken shit into one particular name.
I come back with two Bronze Stars for valor,
Not some damn meritorious Star for typing, the CIB,
And the usual Service ribbons. In Japan, I had my pajamas
Pinned with a Purple Heart. I have no uses for license plates
Saying *Purple Heart.* My wife asked me if I'd like one.
Told her, hell no. You get that for getting killed or being
Like me being near a mine that goes off and blows away
A buddy and does me serious damage. The better, wiser
Thing is to blow up the other guy. Take his eyes. I never
Took my Heart to indicate anything than bad fucking luck.
Men have been wasted because some officer wants promotion.
I got my first Star for not falling back one day in the central
Highlands. I told Top it was because I was getting over
A bad case of the runs and couldn't hustle as fast as my squad.
He told me to keep my mouth shut. Our Captain had a hard on
For medals that made his command look good in daily briefings.
Second Star I got running around shooting up the bastards
One day on a search and destroy. I'll take that one but I have to say
I was nobody's hero; I was mostly pissed off that Mr. Charles
Wouldn't let us get on the slicks and get out of Dodge. We knew
By the time we got back the cold beers waiting wouldn't be cold.

I hate to think of all the young boys I killed just to get my beer.
But they were trying to kill me, so I guess it's all right. I don't
Know what our heroes in Iraq get their Stars for. Don't matter
Much unless you want to be a county commissioner. And, some do.

But about that one name, by the time I was halfway through my tour,
Boots broke in, my shit together, I become focused on being
Focused with any danger to me.

One of the reasons I like John's is we get damn few officer
Types in here. I know you're smart but you keep it to yourself.
See, we had us a new Lt. for one of our operations way out
In the highlands. Totally I-Drang. This guy spooned peaches
Like he was sitting at a table in the White House.

Top told all of us, *Look out. He was going for*
Some tin for the bars in his first three months.
He was our first West Pointer. Rah-rah-sis-boom-bah.
Wanted his war squared away. He wanted good photographs.
Anyways, we deployed in a big circle on some hilltop. Men all dug in.
Some trying to catch some zees before the night. We expected
To get hit. That was the whole point. Everything was all zeroed
In and we cut fire lanes.. Some of us took off our shirts
And put them on sticks to make some shade. When he saw this
He went ape shit, tore the ears off a few sergeants for letting the men
Perform in an unmilitary manner. Then he gave the order to put
Those shirts back on. Well, we were on the opposite side of the circle
And this was a big circle. We were out in company strength, parts
Of our battalion on different hill tops. We even had a few motors.
We was bait but we was loaded bait. Anyway, he come round and sees me
And my fire team, a few others, still with our shirts off. We're writing letters,
improving our positions, and such, but he don't see none of that.

You men, he hollers, *get over here and give me twenty five.*
Right now. When I give an order, by God, I expect it to be followed.
This isn't a picnic. I expect you to look military at all times
So you will be military at all times. Sergeant Doolin, count them out.
And we got out our holes and did the pushups.
Sergeant, he says, *don't let this happen again.*
Yes sir. I say, knowing he was dead but didn't know it.
I wouldn't pull the trigger but several of my boys had that look
In their eyes. Hard orders, yes. Chickenshit, no. There it is.

That night the Major told the Captain who told the Lieutenant
To take a squad out to this little draw that was pointed right
At our positions, set a few claymores and nasty see, nasty do.
The Lt. says he'd take my men out *to redeem* themselves.
He'd be there to make sure they did. You understand
This was ticket punching. Soon enough he'd be back
In Saigon banging reports on a typewriter. It was known
He was the Colonel's fair haired boy, and he worked it.

My beer has lost its chill. Do me a favor and wave your hands
And order me another cold one. Or better, here is some money
Why don't you go get us two cold Buds. I ain't going nowhere.
(In a loud voice) Hey, get some peanuts while you're there.
Thank you kindly. I expect by the time I finish this one
My wife will be here to fetch me home. She is at her beauty
Parlor. It's a right judicious use of time. Life is not to waste.
She teaches school. Always had brains enough for both of us.

Come dark, my squad left the wire to set an ambush,
All taped down, not much to carry. Wasn't nothing for me
To do but wait. It may be a war on but it's still the Army.
Same old, same old. Darker. Dumber. Out of sight. Silence
You could cut with a knife. Cold. Thank God for poncho liners.
Near morning is real quiet. The Congless Cong had refused to
Take the baitless bait. Funny thing about all this is our new Lt.
Didn't make it back to the wire. I report to the Captain
We didn't hear no firefight. Just men and bugs out there.
 The men say they didn't shoot at anything. But nobody knows
Where Lt.Witherspoon is or where he went, or anything.
They were all maintaining silent readiness, you know.
Each man figured the others had him covered.
Just so he wouldn't get them all killed.

Hard men take their time to get tuned in. Fools don't.
He was what you might call a clear and present danger,
I remember that phrase from my civics class. A platoon
Went out to do a rescue or to bring in the body. Nada.
He's on the Wall. A little MIA star by his name.
Somebody in his family got his Purple heart.
The Major was pissed. I had the platoon for a week.
After that things got pretty hot. They say our body count
Made Time magazine. Few weeks later, I was blind.
And now here we sit in John's drinking beer we can't
Buy in Stanly county. We are about the most ridiculous

          People on earth.

MARGINAL NOTES

Fear makes then unmakes the maiden.
Envy keeps a man from living like a King.
*

My love looks over my shoulder.
How can you write such things about me?
Should I explain I am not writing about her?
*

Do you remember those April days when
We knew nothing of beauty in a blemish?
*

I still don't know why you say
Leave the light on but shut your eyes.
*

I don't want a second chance.
Give it to the March of Dimes.
*

The white coat says, *You are depressed*.
Listening to his blather, who wouldn't be?
Bed is my boat; I get sea sick between the sheets.
*

Cum Laude at the University of Girls,
I made *"A"s* with rum and coke, grass too.
A party in tasseled loafers I was no help
The girl who jumped from the Bell Tower.
Over and over in my ear she whispered
I hate to wait. I hate to wait.
*

It is a very good thing
I don't believe in the Rapture.
Lord knows, I am afraid of heights.
*

God loves us but He is easy to piss off.
He kills people to make a point.
He'll end the world by fire.
His face can fry us
He drives the bus.
He is jealous,
Obstinate,
Endless..
*

You know the story:
You finally show your face
And your father celebrates.
You are enjoying a fine blue plate—
Chicken, mashed taters, and green peas
When your high school girl friend
Walks up and says, "When you're done,
Your daughter wants to meet you."
*

Only idiots equate women with angels.
Angels are bodiless spirits and always obey their father.
*

Man is born to hunt.
Look into a hound dog's eyes
And tell me this is blasphemy.
*

I too have seen the best minds of my generation.
They are angry women.
*

Only the brightest poets
Experience *Darkness all the time.*
*

Being old.
Being old is mostly exhaustion
However big your bank.
*

Why, poet, did you enter the dark wood?
Because moonbeams beam better in the dark.
*

Science concerns itself
With unvarnished truth.

Poetry concerns itself
With the truth of varnish.

RIP Robert Watson

WAVES NEVER WAVER

Atlantic Ocean from the outer banks
Talking to itself in great rumbles
Interior monologues of insistent waves
A slow cinema of white caps, close
Pans of foam and spray. The noise of it
A gigantic heart always breaking,
The frames never as consecutive
As they appear to salt bit eyes.

A golden retriever   The man has a pipe.
Trots down the beach.
I can see he has been   He seems to enjoy
Chasing the surf.   Chasing the ocean
              He can't draw much smoke.   Back to Africa.

Sea gulls maybe forty yards offshore
Fly in gracious curves
Indifferent to the implicit slavery
In biological necessity.

Nothing works in   The Atlantic
My father's pipe.   A shroud
              I walk amidst the debris   Earth's wreath
              Of dead things eaten by winged creatures
My eyes feel infected
With distances.
                                          White pain
                                          Sifts through air,
                                          Grit in my joints.

Luster of cracked shell
Hiroshima of periwinkles
Angel wings, and clots
Of sea weed black as blood.

The ocean of my blood:
Low sound from blood circulation
High sound from my nervous system
Every day is anechoic.

These sea gulls
Could be alabaster
Hail stones. Could be   I want the common occurrences.   Dune oats
Anything when energy   More or less.   Would feed
Leaves them dead   Sparrows
On the beach.   If they liked
                                                                        ocean air

How green the sea
To the precocious son
As he leaped for loft
From his tower cell
And did he then wish for
Feathers large enough
To fit his fable.
At least he was not in love
When he took off.

Now from our
Off season room
Comes down the dune steps
My lover, sweet thing
My heartbreak.

Firm muscles
Hard small breasts
That fit my hands
So her nipples harden
To my heartbeats.

Yellow hull
Wrecked rescue boat
Now a haven, ours
For our last hours.
She doesn't read
The beach, so doesn't
See our story there.

Her arms fill up
With driftwood
And other burnable debris
Left by other parties.
A fire in the shelter
Of this old boat.

Her stomach is supple
Not fat, and her belly button
Round as a dime and shines
When I travel down to her
Lush savannah. She says
I am a hungry bear.
Poor fish.

If love
Could move
With the same

Regularity
We would
Have magic.

The Ocean never sleeps or wakes
But sailors do, of all sorts of seas.
I woke this morning with my
Forecastle on fire and my heart
Shouting abandon ship.

If I were younger
I would fear being left behind
By the good life
And a loving girl
I hope will be my wife.
But for some men a moment comes
When the choice is adventure or
Security, and we choose
Not by reason but by fire.

In the tales
Of Kings and
Queens
So
Many
Lancelots,
My dear
Guinevere.

The curse of men
Is that when we get what we want
We do not want it as much. In this
We are closer to Chimpanzees
Than our self-helps books allow.

> The clasp of genitals
> Hard and soft and sweet
> As the Devil's taffy

The warmth of her tongue
On my pleading sex

> Is this not the origin
> Of art? The Greek Kings

The strange mixed scent
Of her breath
When she rises for a kiss

> Were also sailors, sometimes
> Could plot a course, sometimes not.

Mingles with her musk

> Sin

Has changed the way

> Or

I pray and what I pray for,

> Senseless

Sorry Mother Mary.

> We look back at Hoplites and boys
> Undraped on vases and wonder
> At what love or lust drove
> The warrior to his war.

> Passion
> What has
> Either
> To do
> With fate?

As the song goes, *she once was a gooooood friend of mine.*

> But enough
> Can be too much.
> Just ask the guys
> Who drink
> At seaside
> Taverns.

> Christians, yes
> But also Saracens.

Underneath her beach robe
Is Ali Baba's cave.   Pirates always
Protected only by   Pray for more.
A slip of silk
Bought last summer
With her mother
On a jaunt to Paris.

What is lost love I ask myself   years after our last embrace
There by a small fire, shelter by a boat   F   no longer sea worthy,
Enjoying an embrace so deeply sweet   R   I remember it in my bones.
Despite crippled joints, impotence   E   other natural disasters.
No woman should love a man   E   who risks his sense of Being

Just to see if anything of more interest   D   might happen in his life.
                                            O
                                            (O)
                                            M

                        Will   Take
                                            L
                                            O
                                            V
                                            E
                        By   Rip tide.

                                            Far away.

A PRAYER

I have heard that you are present when wood is split.
In the axe too? Have you no Mrs. I Am That I Am?
And if so, what was her maiden name? Is she the one
You miss most in your travels through our souls?
There is no point is there? That hundredth lamb is a meal.
Is it fair to say the difference between *inner* and *outer*
That is man's greatest puzzle is also heresy? My friends
Are loath to say that at times you act like a sociopath.

After many years of prayer I still can't say with certainty
That unity is a path to or away from madness so divine.
Are you a wolf or a swan in the moat around my skin?
We are said to be born in sin. How is my sin doing?
I would do most anything to be a grape inside your goat
Skin bag and still live as a man among men and women.

I keep thinking questions about you are answers.
I don't know them all. My blood ignores argument.
I have sent thousands of Jesus words through it
Like arrows in the wind. Now I am old with hope.
My prayer is simple but as straight as I can make it:
Thank you for today and have mercy on all beings.